Heather,

Enjoy the flavors of
Being a Kid safely.

Kid Approve is for the Kid
Inside us all, Where dessert
comes first!

Dwyane

Kid
Approved
Mom Certified

This book is dedicated to my girls
who bring me more joy everyday.

Bless the food before us
The *Family* beside us
and the *Love* between us

CHILDREN
ARE NOT a
DISTRACTION
FROM MORE
IMPORTANT WORK
THEY ARE
the Most
IMPORTANT WORK
- CS. LEWIS

When I tell you

I Love You

I don't say it
out of habit or to make
conversation. I say it
to remind you that
YOU ARE

the *Best Thing*

that **Ever Happened** to me.

Contents

"I bake ...

what's your

super power?"

Introduction

If you have a child with food allergies you know the struggle, the frustration and anger that a parent goes through from cooking meals at home, to birthday parties and traveling. If you're like me with a full time job and multiple kids with food allergies, it can get rather crazy.

Our latest book **Kid Approved,** is your solution. I have included amazingly tasty recipes that you can make for your child in a short amount of time with easy-to-find ingredients. This is not just a cookbook. **Kid Approved** is a solution guide for you to keep your child safe in a world of fun and wonder. Included is more than just recipes.I've added menus, shopping guides, label reading tips, some of our favorite brands.

I know you will love this book as much as I loved creating it. The time spent with my girls in the kitchen to bring you **Kid Approved** has been priceless. The food thrown away through failed attempts became a laugh. You can trust me when I say that each recipe is Kid Approved and Mom Certified. If even just one of my girls or the neighborhood children turned their nose up, at the recipe it was thrown out. I want you to be confident when you present a gluten and dairy free dish for your child. They will love it and even ask for seconds. You have found the solution to bringing your family back to the supper table and enjoying a meal prepared with LOVE.

Kitchen Rules

Sit up straight

put your napkin in your lap

give every food a try

good manners always

do not talk with your mouth full

eat your vegetables

keep your elbows off the table

USE YOUR INSIDE VOICE

be polite and say please and thank you

chew with your mouth closed

help the cook

excuse yourself before you get up

help clear the table

be thankful for this meal

Take time to do what makes
your soul happy. Like eat chocolate

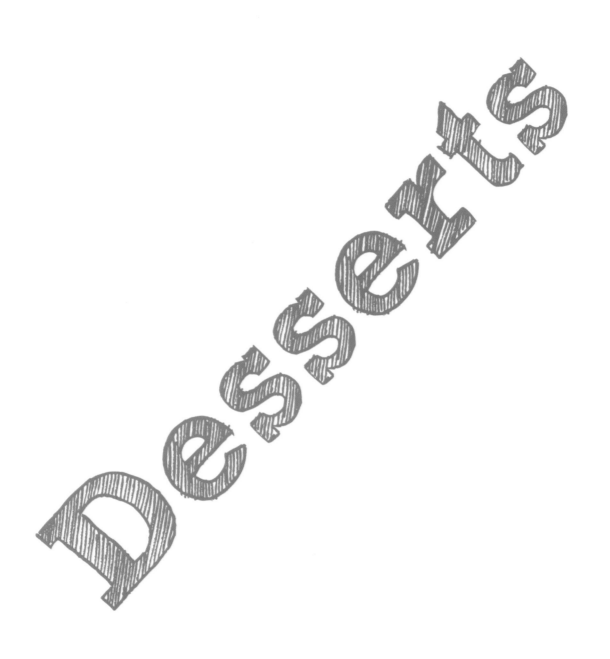

Desserts

dirt pudding

- 2 cups chocolate pudding
- 8 oz whipped topping
- 1 package gluten free chocolate sandwich cookies
- 1 package of 24 gluten free gummy worms

Place the chocolate sandwich cookies in a large zip-top plastic bag, and use a rolling pin to crush them into small pieces. Don't worry about removing the cream filling before putting the cookies in the bag. At first they will clump together, but as you continue to crush them, the cream will blend with the cookies and you won't even notice it.

Continue to crush the cookies in the bag until they are in fine crumbs. A few larger pieces are okay. After all, dirt comes in different sizes!

Add the whipped topping and approximately half of the cookie crumbs to the chocolate pudding. Gently stir everything together until the streaks of whipped topping disappear, and the cookies are well-mixed into the pudding.

Divide the pudding mixture evenly between eight cups. Each should hold a little over ½ cup of pudding. Insert 3 gummy worms into the pudding and press them down a little so that they're embedded. Pour the cookie crumbs over the pudding and gummy worms so that the entire top is covered with "dirt". Smooth it into an even layer with your hands.

snickerdoodle cookies

- 1 cup coconut oil
- 1 1/2 cups sugar
- 2 eggs
- 2 3/4 cups gluten free all purpose flour
- 2 tsp cream of tartar
- 1 tsp baking soda
- 1/4 tsp salt
- 2 tbs sugar
- 2 tsp cinnamon

Preheat oven to 400 degrees.

Line baking sheet with silpat or parchment paper.

Mix thoroughly coconut oil, sugar and eggs. Blend in flour, cream of tartar, salt and baking soda. Refrigerate for 30 minutes.

Mix 2 tablespoons sugar and 2 teaspoons cinnamon in a small bowl.

Shape dough into 1 inch rounded balls. Roll balls in sugar mixture. Place 2 inches apart on ungreased cookie sheet. Bake for 8 to 10 minutes until set. Immediately remove from baking sheet.

angel food cake

- 1 1/2 cups powdered sugar, divided
- 1/3 cup warm water
- 1 cup gluten free all purpose flour
- 1 1/2 tsp cream of tartar
- 1/2 tsp salt
- 1/4 tsp vanilla extract
- 11 egg whites, at room temperature

Preheat oven to 350 degrees.

Sift together flour, salt, and 1/4 cup sugar. In a separate bowl beat the egg whites, water, cream of tartar and vanilla on low speed. Increase the speed. As soon as whites reach the soft-peak stage, begin adding remaining sugar, a tablespoon at a time. Beat until whites are glossy and stiff.

Sift the dry ingredients 1/4 cup at a time over the whites, folding them in after each addition.

Spoon batter into a 10 inch ungreased angel food cake tube pan. (Do not use a pan with a no-stick surface and do not grease the pan) Tap the pan once on the counter to help distribute batter. Place pan on the middle rack of oven and bake 45 minutes.

Edges will pull away from the sides of the pan. Place cake (still in the pan) upside down on a rack. Do not remove cake from the pan for one hour.

notes: do not use a plastic bowl or spoon in preparation

devils food cake

- 1 3/4 cups gluten free all purpose flour
- 4 1/2 tbs cornstarch
- 1 tsp baking powde
- 1/2 tsp baking sodar
- 1 1/4 cups cocoa powder
- 1 tsp salt
- 1 cup unsalted butter
- 2 3/4 cups sugar
- 5 large eggs
- 1 1/4 cup coconut milk
- 1 tbs lemon juice

Preheat oven to 350 degrees. Butter and lightly flour the sides of two 9-inch circle pans, knocking out the excess flour. Do the same to the bottom of the pans or line with parchment paper cut to fit.

Sift together the flour, cornstarch, baking powder, baking soda, cocoa powder, and salt into a bowl and set aside. Add the lemon juice to the milk and set aside.

In the bowl of a stand mixer fitted with the paddle attachment, beat the butter on medium-high speed until light and creamy. Slowly add the sugar and continue to beat until light in color and fluffy. Add the eggs one at a time, mixing well after each before adding the next egg. Stop the mixer and scrape down the sides. With the mixer on low, add the flour mixture in 3 equal batches alternating with the milk mixture, beginning and ending with the flour mixture. Stop the mixer and scrape down the sides, then mix again for a few seconds.

Divide the cake batter between the prepared pans. Bake until the top springs back when lightly touched, or when toothpick comes out clean, about 45 minutes.

Let cakes cool in pans on wire rack. When completely cool, turn them out.

chocolate cake

- 1 1/2 cups rice flour
- 1 cup cocoa powder
- 1 tbs baking powder
- 1/4 cup potato starch
- 2 cups sugar
- 1/2 tsp sea salt
- 1/2 cup water
- 3/4 cup coconut oil, melted
- 4 eggs

Preheat oven to 350 degrees.

Mix rice flour, cocoa powder, baking powder, potato starch, sugar and salt. Stir with a wire whisk until well combined. Add coconut oil, eggs and water; combine until well mixed. Pour into two 9-inch round baking pans that are well greased.

Bake for 25 minutes or until tooth pick in middle comes out clean.

yellow cupcakes

- 2 3/4 gluten free all purpose flour
- 2 tbs baking powder
- 1/2 tsp salt
- 2/3 cup coconut oil, melted
- 4 eggs
- 2 tsp vanilla extract

Preheat oven to 350 degrees. Line cupcake pan with paper liners.

In a medium bowl sift together flour, baking powder and salt.

In a large bowl, combine coconut oil, eggs and vanilla until well mixed. Add flour mixture and combine.

Pour into cupcake liners. Bake for 20 minutes or until top of cupcakes are firm to the touch.

Remove from cupcake pan and cool on wire rack for at least 30 minutes before frosting.

vegan
velvet cake

- 2 cups gluten free all purpose flour
- 1 cup sugar
- 2 tsp baking powder
- 1 tsp baking soda
- 1/2 tsp salt
- 1 tbs egg replacer
- 2 tbs cocoa powder
- 1 tsp vanilla extract
- 1 cup almond milk
- 1 tbs apple cider vinegar
- 1/2 cup cold coffee
- 1/2 cup grape seed oil
- 2 tbs red food coloring

Preheat oven to 325 degrees. Prepare bundt pan or 2 8-inch round cake pans, by rubbing with coconut oil and then coating with flour. Shake and remove the excess.

In a large mixing bowl, whisk together all dry ingredients and set aside. In a medium bowl, mix together all remaining ingredients and food coloring, if using.

Make a well in the middle of the dry ingredients and slowly pour the wet mixture into the well. Slowly whisk together until well mixed, then beat for 1 minute to ensure the cake batter is completely combined. Pour the batter evenly into the prepared pans.

Bake for 30 minutes without opening the oven door. Check the cake and rotate 180 degrees. Bake for another 10 minutes until the top bounces back when touched and a toothpick comes out clean when inserted into the center.

Remove from the oven and let cool on cooling rack for 15 minutes. Invert pans on cooling rack to remove from the pans. Let cakes cool completely, then frost with cream cheese icing or vanilla buttercream.

banana split

- 1 banana, peeled and split lengthwise
- 3 scoops ice cream
- 2 tbs sliced fresh strawberries
- 2 tbs pineapple chunks
- 2 tbs whipped cream
- 1 tbs chopped peanuts
- 1 tbs chocolate syrup
- 2 maraschino cherries with stems

Place banana in a dessert dish. Place scoops of ice cream between banana. Top with remaining ingredients. Serve immediately.

vanilla
ice cream

- 1 cup unsweetened coconut milk
- 3 egg yolks, beaten
- 1 tbs vanilla
- 1/2 cup honey
- 1/4 tsp sea salt
- 2 cups canned coconut milk

In a small saucepan mix the honey, salt, unsweetened coconut milk and egg yolks. Cook over medium heat, stirring constantly until bubbles appear around the edge of the mixture.

Remove from heat and cool to room temperature.

Stir vanilla and canned coconut milk into cooled mixture.

Pour into ice cream maker. Follow ice cream maker instructions.

chocolate syrup

- 2 1/4 cups sugar
- 3/4 cup cocoa powder
- 1 1/2 tbs corn starch
- 1/4 tsp salt
- 1 1/2 cups canned coconut milk
- 1 tbs vanilla

Place first four (dry) ingredients in a medium-sized saucepan, along with 1/2 cup of the coconut milk and whisk to combine into a thick paste.

Add the remaining coconut milk, bringing the mixture to a boil, and whisk to combine well. When sauce boils, reduce heat to low and simmer very gently for 5 minutes, whisking often. Remove from heat. Add vanilla, and cool.

Store in refrigerator for up to 2 weeks, covered.

chocolate frosting

- 4 cups powdered sugar
- 1 cup cocoa powder
- 3 sticks of butter, softened
- 1/4 tsp salt
- 1/2 cup almond milk

In a small bowl, combine powder sugar, cocoa powder and salt until well mixed using a wire whisk. Add butter and combine with electric mixer. Add almond milk to make the dough creamy and spreadable.

buttercream frosting

- 1/2 cup coconut oil
- 1/2 cup shortening
- 2 tsp vanilla extract
- 4 cups powdered sugar
- 1/4 cup coconut milk
- food coloring (optional)

Cream coconut oil and shortening. Add vanilla. Slowly add powdered sugar and then coconut milk in small amounts until it is well mixed. If it gets too stiff, add more coconut milk and mix until smooth and creamy.

apple crisp

- 8 mediium apples, peeled and sliced
- 3/4 cup sugar
- 1/2 tsp ground cinnamon
- 1/8 tsp salt

Toppings
- 1/2 cup gluten free oats
- 1/2 cup gluten free all purpose flour
- 1/2 cup brown sugar
- 1/4 tsp baking powder
- 1/8 tsp baking soda
- 3 tbs cold butter or coconut oil

In a large bowl, toss the first four ingredients. Pour into a greased 8 inch square baking dish.

In a bowl, combine oats, flour, brown sugar, baking powder and baking soda. Cut in butter until mixture resembles coarse crumbs. Sprinkle over apple mixture.

Bake at 350 degrees for 55 - 60 minutes or until apples are tender.

Serve warm.

chocolate pudding

- 1/4 cup sugar
- 1/4 cup unsweetened cocoa powder
- 2 tbs cornstarch
- 1/8 tsp salt
- 2 cups coconut milk
- 1 egg
- 1/2 cup chocolate chips

Whisk together the sugar, cocoa powder, cornstarch and salt in a heavy 2-quart saucepan. Gradually whisk in the coconut milk. Bring to a boil, whisking constantly. Boil while whisking until the pudding is thick, about 4 minutes. Remove from heat.

Immediately beat the egg lightly in a medium, heat proof bowl, such as a hard pastic or ceramic mixing bowl. Very gradually add the hot chocolate mixture to the egg, whisking constantly.

Whisk in the chocolate chips until they are melted and the mixture is smooth. Pour into pudding cups.

Cover with plastic wrap, pressing the plastic to the surface to prevent the pudding from forming a film and refrigerate until cold, at least 2 hours.

oatmeal cookies

- 1 cup coconut oil
- 2 cups sugar
- 1 tbs molasses
- 2 eggs
- 1 1/2 tsp vanilla
- 4 cups gluten free rolled oats
- 2 tbs almond milk
- 1 tsp baking soda
- 1/2 tsp salt
- 2 cups gluten free all purpose flour
- 1 cup raisins

Mix melted coconut oil and sugar together giving time for the sugar to melt. Add eggs, molasses, vanilla, milk and mix well. Sift together flour, baking soda, salt and mix into liquid mixture. Add oats and raisins. Mix till well combined.

Preheat oven to 375 degrees. Scoop 1 tbs cookie dough onto baking sheet lined with silpat leaving 2 inches between cookies. Bake for 10 minutes. Remove from pan and cool. Cookies will appear slightly soft when done.

oat cream sandwiches

- 1 batch oatmeal cookies
- 1/2 gallon dairy free ice cream

Pair the completely cooled cookies with like-size mates. Slightly soften the ice cream. Sandwich a scoop of ice cream between each set of cookie bottoms. Press gently to squeeze the ice cream slightly beyond the edges. Use a small offset spatula to smooth the ice cream flush with the cookies. Wrap in wax paper. Freeze until very firm, at least 2 hours.

graham crackers

- 1/2 cup + 2 tbs potato flour
- 1/3 cup + 1 tbs brown rice flour
- 1/3 cup tapioca flour
- 1/3 cup + 2 tbs white rice flour
- 1 tsp cinnamon
- 1 tsp baking powder
- 1/2 tsp xantham gum
- 1/2 tsp salt
- 7 tbs coconut oil
- 1/4 cup honey
- 3 to 6 tbs cold water

Preheat oven to 325 degrees.

Line a baking sheet with silpat or parchment paper.

Add dry ingredients to large bowl, cut in coconut oil. The dough will look like crumbs. Mix in honey. Add cold water slowly until a dough forms.

Roll out on surface covered in rice flour to 1/4 inch. Cut into squares or rectangles. Bake until firm on baking sheet.

franki freezes

- 1 cup boiling water
- 2 cups sprite
- 1 flavored Jello

Into a square cake pan, whisk the Jello into the boiling water until dissolved. Stir in the soda pop. Freeze for at least 4 hours or overnight. Use a cookie or ice cream scoop to shave the ice. Serve immediately.

blueberry
kefir popsicles

- 1 1/2 cups vanilla kefir
- 1 tbs honey
- 1 cup fresh blueberries

Mix the kefir and honey in a small bowl. Smash blueberries, add and mix well. Pour into popsicle molds and freeze.

Host your own little baker party!

Supplies:
unfrosted cupcakes
frosting
sprinkles
plastic cocktail cups
cupcake wrappers (FREE Download)
plastic cellophane bags
ribbon

Instructions:
Make the cupcakes and frosting up ahead of time. I used GF Mom Certified Vanilla Bean and Buttercream Frosting recipes. You can get the cupcake wrappers, cellophane bags, ribbon, clear plastic cocktail cups and sprinkles from your dollar store to save. I found the cupcake cellophane bags at our local Dollar Tree.

Once the little baker is done decorating, drop a Sweet Cakes cupcake wrapper in a cocktail cup. Drop in the decorated cupcake carefully. Place in a cellophane bag and tie shut with ribbon. All ready to take home!

Birthday Solutions

Taking your gluten free child to a birthday party is scary. The anxiety starts the day you receive the invite. The initial thoughts I have are, _where_ is the party? _Who_ is hosting? _What_ are they serving? Is there going to be cake? (THERE WILL BE CAKE!) _What_ about ice cream? _What_ about the favors? Maybe I should just decline? I am sure if you have a child with food allergies you have the same reaction and questions. I know I am not the only one, as I hear the same fear from other parents.

Today I am going to give you a few tips for when your child is attending a birthday party.

1. BYOC...Bring your own Cupcake

2. Call Ahead - Call the host of the party and share your child's allergies. The idea is not to scare the host and get your child uninvited. The idea is to be vocal and share your story in order to create awareness and lessen concerns. I always let them know our girls cannot have gluten or dairy including bread, cake, pizza, or ice cream.

3. Pack your child a snack or meal for the party and label it clearly with gluten free labels or stickers. I will pre-cook and pack pizza for pizza parties. We bring dairy-free ice cream, with extra in case another child with allergies forgot. I have also brought our own hotdogs and pretzels. You can even bring enough gluten free pretzels or chips to share.

4. Pack your Epi pen and notify parents at the party of your child's allergies and reactions, as you may not always be present. Yes, your child will run and play with the other kids. With Lillie's peanut allergy we have to make sure if someone see's her turning red or coughing they alert an adult immediately.

5. Talk with your child prior to and on the way to the party. I will reiterate,I have packed her pizza and caketo bring to the party. Remind your child not to eat any of the party food so they do not get sick or their tummy won't hurt. Communication is key.

birthday party menu

Kid friendly menu includes:

- celery and carrots in cocktail cups with ranch dressing on the bottom
- carrot chips served in cupcake wrappers
- veggie straws in wax paper cones
- popcorn in wax paper cones
- water bottles and juice boxes
- gluten free pretzels in small plastic bags
- fruit kabobs (grapes, pineapple, cantaloupe, watermelon, strawberries)
- crab shaped gluten free sugar cookies in clear plastic bags

All food will be packaged with party labels to make it easy for the kids to walk around or take outside. The drinks will be in buckets of ice outside on the patio.

Table Layout

candyland party menu

Kid friendly menu includes:
- mini cupcakes - chocolate and vanilla bean
- lollipop sugar cookies
- fruit lollipops
- popcorn 3 ways
- marshmallow lollipops
- lollipops
- smartie candy
- strawberry punch
- strawberry gelato

I licked it,

so it's mine

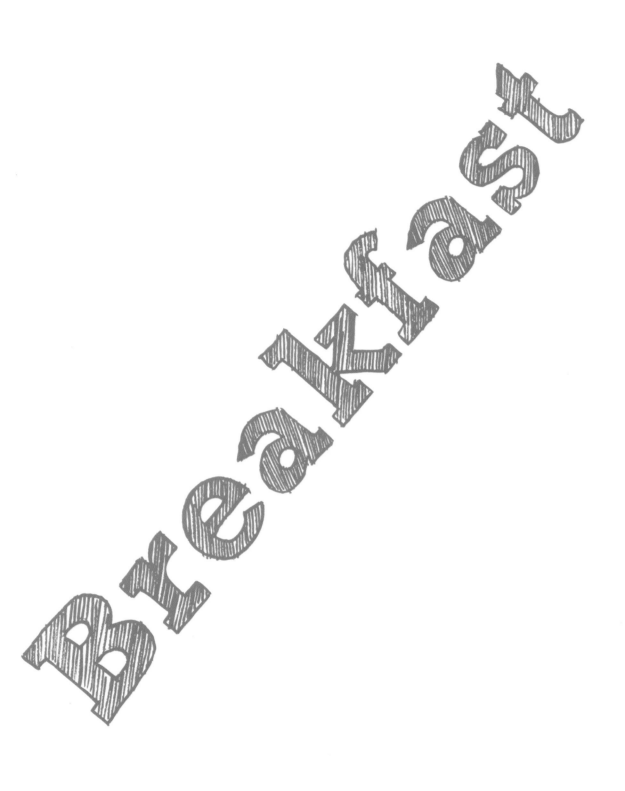

josi juice

- 1 cucumber
- 2 celery stalks
- 2 whole carrots
- 1 orange, peeled
- 1 green apple, cored
- 1 sweet potato, peeled

Run all ingredients through a juicer. Serve over ice.

strawberry donuts

- 2 cups gluten free all purpose flour
- 3/4 cup sugar
- 1 tsp baking powder
- 1 tsp baking soda
- 1 tsp kosher salt
- 2 tsp vanilla extract
- 2 eggs
- 3/4 cup almond milk
- 2 tbs butter, melted

Glaze
- 1/2 cup canned coconut milk
- 2 tsp vanilla extract
- 4 1/2 cups powdered sugar
- 1 tbs strawberry gelatin powder
- sprinkles, optional

In a large mixing bowl, combine all donut ingredients until well blended. Fill a donut pan 1/2-3/4 full with batter. I like to put my batter in a large ziploc bag and snip off the corner. Makes filling the donut pan much easier (and cleaner). Bake donuts in a 325 degree oven for about 12 minutes. Remove. Cool on wire rack for 5 minutes, remove from pan and cool completely before glazing.

While donuts are baking, add coconut milk and vanilla to a medium sized saucepan over medium-low heat. Stir and heat until warm. Whisk in the gelatin mix and slowly whisk in powdered sugar. Remove from heat.

To glaze donuts, either dip donut tops into glaze and immediately add sprinkles. Or, using a large spatula, spread glaze on top of donuts and add sprinkles, if desired. Allow to set, about 5-10 minutes.

fruit smoothie

- 1 banana, peeled
- 8 strawberries, hulled
- 1 orange, peeled
- 1/2 cup kefir
- 6 ice cubes

In a blender combine banana, strawberries, orange and yogurt. Toss in the ice. Blend until smooth and creamy. Pour into glasses and serve.

oatmeal

- 2 cups water
- 1/4 tsp salt
- 3/4 cup gluten free rolled oats

Mix Ins
- cinnamon
- sugar
- brown sugar
- blueberries
- raisins
- apple butter
- strawberry jam

Bring water and salt to a boil. Add oats and continue simmering for about 5 minutes. Stir to desired thickness.

overnight groats

- 4 cups gluten free groats
- 8 cups water
- 2 tsp cinnamon
- 1 tsp vanilla extract
- 1 cup dried cranberries
- 1 cup pecan halves
- 1/4 cup pure maple syrup

Combine the oats, water, cinnamon, pecans and vanilla extract in a slow cooker.

Cook on low for 8 hours.

Stir in the cranberries and maple syrup when serving.

scrambled eggs

- 4 eggs
- 1/4 cup shredded cheese
- 1/4 cup chopped ham
- 2 tsp butter or bacon grease

Beat eggs in bowl until blended.

Heat butter in a large skillet over medium heat until eggs begin to set. Add in ham and cheese. Gently pull the eggs across the pan with a spatula, forming large soft curds.

Continue cooking by pulling, lifting and folding eggs until thickened and still soft. Do not stir constantly. Remove from heat. Serve immediately.

hard boiled eggs

• eggs

Place eggs in saucepan large enough to hold them in single layer. ADD cold water to cover eggs by 1 inch. Heat over high heat just to boiling. Remove from burner. Cover pan.

Let eggs stand in hot water about 12 minutes for large eggs; 9 minutes for medium eggs; 15 minutes for extra large.

Drain immediately and serve warm. Or, cool completely under cold running water or in bowl of ice water, then refrigerate.

kefir parfaits

- 2 cups vanilla kefir
- 1 1/2 cups gluten free granola
- 1 cup berries, chopped
  strawberries
  blueberries
  raspberries
  blackberries

In 4 parfait cups or shot glasses layer kefir, granola, berries of your choice and repeat.

Chill in refrigerator until ready to eat. Can be stored overnight in air tight container.

banana muffins

- 2 cups gluten free all purpose flour
- 1 tsp baking soda
- 1/8 tsp salt
- 1/2 cup oil
- 3/4 cup sugar
- 1/4 cup brown sugar, packed
- 2 eggs
- 3 ripe bananas, mashed
- 1/2 tsp vanilla extract

Heat oven to 325 degrees. Line muffin pan with paper liners.

In a medium size bowl, sift together the flour, baking soda and salt. Set aside. In a large mixing bowl mix together the oil and sugars. Add eggs, mashed bananas and vanilla, stirring until well blended. Fold in the dry ingredients.

Pour batter into prepared muffin cups and bake for 35 - 45 minutes or until toothpick inserted in center comes out clean. Transfer muffins to wire rack to cool before serving.

cinnamon apple streusel muffins

- 2 cups gluten free all purpose flour
- 1/2 cup brown sugar
- 1/4 cup sugar
- 2 tsp baking powder
- 1 tsp baking soda
- 1/2 tsp salt
- 1 tbs egg replacer
- 1 tsp cinnamon
- 1/4 tsp nutmeg
- 3/4 cup almond milk
- 1/3 cup apple sauce
- 1 tbs apple cider vinegar

Streusel Topping
- 1/4 cup gluten free all purpose flour
- 1/3 cup brown sugar
- 2 tsp cinnamon
- 3 tbs coconut oil, soft

Preheat oven to 350 degrees. Lightly grease or line a muffin pan.

In a large bowl, whisk together all of the dry ingredients.

In a medium bowl, combine the wet ingredients.

Make a well in the middle of the dry ingredients and pour in the milk mixture. Stir with a wooden spoon. Pour the batter into the muffin pan.

Combine the ingredients for the streusel topping and sprinkle it evenly on the batter.

Bake for 22 to 25 minutes or until a knife comes out clean when inserted. Allow to cool slightly before removing from the muffin tins. Cool on a wire rack.

french toast

- 1 tsp ground cinnamon
- 1/4 tsp ground nutmeg
- 2 tbs sugar
- 4 tbs coconut oil
- 4 eggs
- 1/4 cup almond milk
- 1/2 tsp vanilla extract
- 8 slices gluten free white bread
- 1/2 cup gluten free maple syrup, warmed

In a small bowl combine cinnamon, nutmeg, and sugar. Set aside briefly.

In a 10-inch or 12-inch skillet, melt coconut oil over medium heat. Whisk together cinnamon mixture, eggs, almond milk, and vanilla and pour into a shallow container such as a pie plate. Dip bread in egg mixture. Fry slices until golden brown, then flip to cook the other side. Serve with syrup.

nickle
flaps

- 3/4 cup white rice flour
- 3/4 cup corn starch
- 3/4 cups almond flour
- 1 1/2 cups alomond milk
- 2 tbs sugar
- 2 eggs
- 1/2 tsp vanilla
- 3 tbs coconut oil, melted
- 2 tsp baking powder
- 1/2 tsp salt

Mix all ingredients until well combined.

Heat griddle pan over medium-high heat. Pour pancake mix 1 tablespoon at a time on hot griddle. Flip pancake when you see bubbles form on the surface. Cook other side until lightly golden.

Serve warm.

sweet potato pancakes

- 1 cup white rice flour
- 1/2 cup sweet potato flour
- 1/2 cup potato starch
- 1/4 cup tapioca starch
- 1 tbs baking powder
- 1/2 tsp salt
- 1/4 cup sugar
- 2 1/4 cups almond milk
- 2 eggs or egg replacer
- 1/4 cup oil

Add white rice flour, sweet potato flour, potato starch, tapioca starch, baking powder, salt, and sugar to a medium bowl and mix with a wire whisk. Add milk, eggs (or replacer), and oil. Stir until well blended. The batter should be the consistency of a thin cake batter.

Pour batter into small circles onto preheated griddle. Use a well seasoned griddle and do not oil the surface.

Cook over medium heat. When the pancake begins to form air bubbles that rise to the top, it is time to turn the pancake over. Allow to cook until the inside of the pancake is fully cooked. Remove from pan.

If you stack them as you cook, the pancakes will remain hot longer. Serve with warm cinnamon apples.

Do not be afraid to add more milk to thin out the batter. The batter should be a little on the thin side.

mini quiche cups

- 4 eggs
- 1 cup almond milk
- 1 1/2 cups ham, chopped
- 1 1/2 cups aged cheddar cheese, diced
- 1 cup broccoli, chopped
- 1/2 tsp ground mustard
- 1/2 tsp sea salt
- 1/4 tsp black pepper

Heat oven to 375 degrees. Line cupcake pan with silpat liners.

Layer ham, cheese and broccoli in each cupcake liner.

In medium bowl, beat eggs and milk with fork. Stir in remaining ingredients. Pour over broccoli.

Bake 25 minutes or until knife inserted in center comes out clean.

Let stand 5 to 10 minutes before serving.

Be bold enough to use your voice brave enough to listen to your heart, and strong enough to live the life you've always imagined.

pecola's granola rola

- 1/2 cup brown sugar
- 1/2 cup honey
- 1/4 cup coconut oil
- 4 cups old fashioned oats
- 1/2 tsp cinnamon
- 1/4 tsp salt
- 1/2 cup raisins (optional)
- 1/2 cup almond slivers (optional)
- 1/2 cup coconut flakes (optional)
- 1/2 cup chocolate chips (optional)

Preheat oven to 250 degrees.

Combine brown sugar, honey and coconut oil in a small sauce pan over medium heat.

Cook, stirring often until sugar is dissolved.

Pour brown sugar mixture over oats and add cinnamon and salt. Stir until oats are evenly coated. Add in raisins, almonds, coconut flakes and chocolate chips (optional).

Spread granola mixture over a cookie sheet lined with silpat and press mixture down.

Place in oven and bake for 1 hour, stirring every 15-20 minutes.

Remove from oven and allow to cool completely before breaking apart and into pieces.

Store in air tight container.

holy kale chips

- 1 bunch kale
- olive oil
- sea salt

Preheat oven to 400 degrees.

Wash, trim stems and pat dry kale leaves.

Lay kale out on baking sheet. Do not overlap. Drizzle with olive oil and sea salt. Bake for 4 minutes.

Kale burns quickly, so watch it. The chips are ready when the edges are a little brown.

soft pretzels

- 2 3/4 cups gluten free all purpose flour
- 1 tsp salt
- 1 tsp sugar
- 1 package active dry yeast (1/4 oz) *fast rising or regular will work fine*
- 1 cup warm water plus about 3 tbs more

Baking Soda Wash
- 1/8 cup warm water
- 2 tsp. baking soda
- 3 tbs butter (optional)
- kosher or sea salt (course)

Preheat oven to 500 degrees.

Put all of the dough ingredients into a bowl and mix well, forming a nice dough and then knead for at least 5 minutes. The dough should be very smooth, soft and pliable. When it is ready, just pat into a ball and place it in a glass bowl that has been lightly coated with olive oil. Cover with cling wrap and put in microwave using our rising secret. Let rise to double the size (takes about 40 minutes to an hour).

Take the dough and roll it into a thick log and cut into 8 equal parts. Roll into lengths of about 10 inches and form your pretzels. Make your baking soda wash. Add the warm water to the baking soda and mix well. Brush the wash over the outside of the pretzel and repeat for all of them. Pop them in the oven and cook for 9 minutes. They should be a rich pretzel brown.

Remove from the oven. Melt your butter and apply to all of the pretzels and sprinkle with salt.

fresh
salsa

- 3 tomatoes, chopped
- 1/2 onion, chopped
- 1 tsp sea salt
- 1 bunch cilantro, chopped
- 1 tbs olive oil
- 1 cup sweet corn (optional)

Mix all ingredients together in a small bowl.

Allow to sit for 5 minutes before serving.

Store covered in refrigerator for up to 2 days.

fruit
kabobs

- 1 lb strawberries
- 1 bunch seedless grapes
- 1 watermelon
- 1 canteloupe
- 1 pint blueberries
- 1 pineapple

Cube up the fruit and get your kids involved to make these fruit kabobs for your next event!

Cube fruit and place on skewers.

Store in the refrigerator covered until ready to eat.

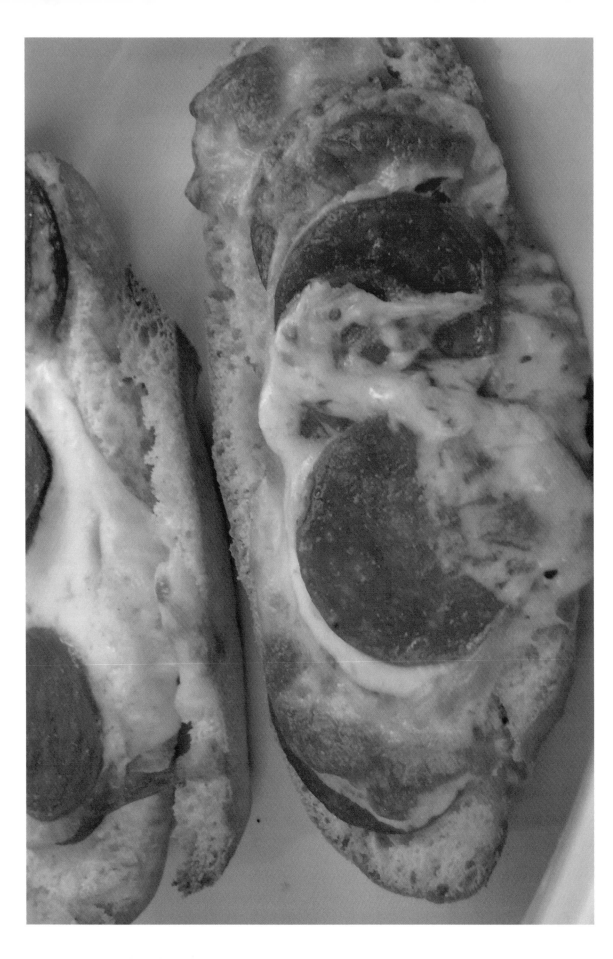

pizza
bread

- 1 loaf of gluten free french bread
- 2 tbs olive oil
- 1 clove garlic
- 1 large ball of fresh mozarella cheese
- pepperoni

Split the loaf first lengthwise and then across into 4 sections. Toast bread lightly under broiler for 5 minutes. Remove from broiler. Top with olive oil, rub with garlic. Top with cheese and pepperoni. Return the bread to the broiler until the cheese browns and bubbles. Remove pizza from the oven and serve.

Snack Ideas

APPLE STICKS & NUT BUTTER
BANANAS
BROWNIES
CARROT STICKS
CELERY STICKS & NUT BUTTER
CLEMENTINES
COOKIES
DRY CEREAL
FROZEN FRUIT BITES
GRANOLA
MUFFINS
POPCORN
POPSICLE SMOOTHIES
SALAMI & CRACKERS
STRAWBERRIES & CHOCOLATE
TORTILLA CHIPS & SALSA
YOUGURT & FRUIT

the question
isn't who is
going to let me;
it's who is going
to stop me.

- ayn Rand

DADS

World Famous

BBQ

daddy's bbq
menu

Menu:
- Corn on the Cob
- French Onion Burgers (pg. 21 GF Mom Certified)
- Hot Dogs
- Chips and Salsa
- Cucumber Punch
- Mac & Cheese (GF elbow mac and Cabot Cheese)
- Coconut Ice Cream
- Strawberry Cake with Vanilla Icing (pg. 61 of GF Mom Certified)
- Fruit Kabobs (strawberry, pineapple, cantaloupe, grape, watermelon)
- *Local Oven* Onion Buns and Hot Dog Buns (GF)

chicken fingers

- 2 chicken breasts
- 1 egg
- 1/4 cup brown rice flour
- 1/4 cup gluten free bread crumbs
- 1/2 cup corn meal or cracked corn
- 1 tbs mom certified spice

Preheat oven to 450 degrees.

Cut chicken into bites, then beat with a meat hammer to break down. If needed, cut nuggets in half after beating to smaller size.

Put chicken nuggets into medium bowl, add egg and mix well.

In a shallow dish or bowl, mix together brown rice flour, bread crumbs, corn meal and mom certified spice.

Dredge egg covered chicken through dry mixture. Place in baking pan and bake for 25 minutes or until chicken is done.

pizza

- 4 1/2 cups gluten free all purpose flour
- 400 ml warm water, 110 degrees
- 2 tbs fresh yeast or 1 pkg dry yeast
- 2 tsp sugar
- 3 tbs olive oil
- 1/2 tsp garlic
- 1/4 tsp oregano
- 1/2 tsp basil

Toppings
- gluten free pizza sauce
- 1/8 cup onion, diced
- 1/8 cup green pepper, diced
- 1 roma tomato, sliced
- pepperoni
- canadian bacon
- 1 fresh mozarella ball
- 1 cup shredded mozarella
- 1/2 tsp dried oregano

Add sugar and yeast, crumbled to warm water. Allow to sit for 10 minutes.

Using stand mixer with hook attachment. Add all ingredients mixing on low until the dough forms. Then beat on medium-high for 3-5 minutes to knead dough.

Coat dough with olive oil and allow to rise in warm humid place for 40 minutes.

Preheat oven to 400 degrees. Punch down and roll out into thin pizza crust. Makes 3 pizzas.

Cook at 400 degrees for 12 minutes to pre-bake crust. Add ingredients then cook 15 - 20 minutes until cheese starts to brown.

the lillie
pizza

- 4 1/2 cups gluten free all purpose flour
- 400 ml warm water, 110 degrees
- 2 tbs fresh yeast or 1 pkg dry yeast
- 2 tsp sugar
- 3 tbs olive oil
- 1/2 tsp garlic
- 1/4 tsp oregano
- 1/2 tsp basil

Toppings
- garlic oil
- pepperoni
- candian bacon
- buffalo mozarella

Add sugar and yeast, crumbled, to warm water. Allow to sit for 10 minutes.

Using stand mixer with hook attachment. Add all ingredients mixing on low until the dough forms. Then beat on medium-high for 3-5 minutes to knead dough.

Coat dough with olive oil and allow to rise in warm humid place for 40 minutes.

Preheat oven to 400 degrees. Punch down and roll out into thin pizza crust. Make 3 pizzas.

Cook at 400 degrees for 12 minutes to pre-bake crust. Add ingredients then cook 15 - 20 minutes until cheese starts to brown.

thin crust pizza

- 1 cup white rice flour
- 1 cup brown rice flour
- 1 cup tapioca flour
- 3/4 tsp xanthan gum
- 1 tsp salt
- 1 tsp oregano
- 1 tsp basil
- 1 tsp garlic
- 1/2 tsp baking powder
- 2 tbs sugar
- 1 1/4 cup warm water
- 1 tbs olive oil

Preheat oven to 350 degrees.

In a medium bowl, combine gluten free flours, xanthan gum, salt, baking powder, oregano, basil, garlic, and sugar. Whisk until well combined.

Make a well in the dry mixture and add the water. Add the olive oil before stirring. Then stir it all together until well combined, using a wooden spoon.

Lightly coat a baking sheet or pizza stone with non-stick spray and plop your dough down. Using a spoon or spatula, work from the middle and push to spread/flatten the dough out to the edge. Spread pretty thin - less than 1/4 inch.

Put the pizza in the oven to pre-bake for roughly 25-30 minutes, or until it begins to look dry. Cracks may appear, but that's normal.

Remove from oven and spread generously with your favorite pizza sauce, cheese and desired toppings. Pop back in oven for another 20-25 minutes, or until the crust edge looks golden brown and the toppings are warm and bubbly.

Cut immediately and serve. Reheats well the next day in the oven or microwave.

bacon burgers

- 8 bacon slices
- 2 lbs ground sirloin
- 1 tbs ground cumin
- 1 tbs chili powder
- 2 tbs steak seasoning
- 2 tsp ground coriander
- 2 garlic cloves, finely chopped
- 1 tbs olive oil
- 4 gluten free buns
- 4 slices of aged cheese
- 1 sweet onion, sliced (optional)

Preheat grill to medium hot.

Heat a skillet over medium-high heat. Add bacon to the pan and cook until cripsy, 8 to 10 minutes. Move bacon to a paper towel lined plate to drain. Add sliced onion to skillet if you wish to have grilled onions for burgers.

In a medium bowl, combine the ground meat with cumin, chili powder, steak seasoning, coriander and garlic. Form four large patties about 1 inch thick. Make a shallow indentation at the center of the patties to prevent the burgers from bulging as they cook. Coat the burgers with 1 tablespoon olive oil to prevent sticking.

Grill the burgers for 10 minutes, turning once for medium.

Place each burger on a bun and top with cheese, bacon slices and onions (optional).

pretzel dogs

- 3/4 cup almond milk
- 1/4 cup water
- 1 1/2 tbs sugar
- 1 pkg active dry yeast
- 2 cups gluten free all purpose flour
- 2 tbs coconut oil, softened
- 1 tsp sea salt
- 8 frozen hot dogs
- 3 cups hot water
- 1/2 cup baking soda
- 1 egg, beaten
- 1 tbs water
- sea salt

Combine almond milk, water and sugar in a sauce pan and heat on low until the temp is 110 degrees.

Pour warm mixture into stand mixer bowl. Sprinkle yeast on top and allow to sit for 5 minutes.

In a medium bowl combine flour, salt and coconut oil.

Using the dough hook attachment on the stand mixer, slowly add flour into yeast mixture while mixing on slow. Continue on slow until all ingredients are combined and then crank up the speed to medium for about 8 minutes. Once the dough is smooth and looks like a thick cake batter cover with oil and place in a warm humid place to rise for 1 hour.

Preheat oven to 450 degrees.

Punch down pretzel dough and divide into 8 even balls. Remove hotdogs from freezer. Roll out dough into a long snake, like you would with play dough. Wrap each dough snake around each hot dog.

Mix water with baking soda into a deep dish big enough to submerge the hot dogs. Dip each hot dog for 15 seconds. Place hotdogs on baking sheet lined with silpat 2 inches apart. Combine egg and water in small bowl and brush on pretzels. Sprinkle with salt. Bake for 15 minutes or until golden brown. Remove to cooling rack until cool enough to handle. Serve hot.

french
fries

- 5 large potatoes
- 1/2 tsp onion powder
- 1/2 tsp garlic powder
- 2 tbs grapeseed oil
- sea salt

Soak sliced potatoes in cold water for 10 minutes to remove the excess starch.

Cook on cookie sheet drizzled with grape seed oil and salt.

Cook for 15 minutes on the lowest rack of your oven at the broil setting.

Season now with onion or garlic powder.

Finish in the broiler for 2 minutes - watch fries close so they do not burn.

mac and cheese

- 2 cups water
- 2 cups rice milk
- 1 box gluten free macaroni
- 2 cups gluten free, lactose free cheese, shredded
- 1 tbs dijon mustard

Bring water and milk to a boil in a 2 quart pan. Add macaroni and cook for 8 minutes. Then stir in shredded cheese and dijon mustard, until cheese is all melted.

Allow to sit for 5 minutes before serving.

burritos

- 2 lbs ground beef
- 1/2 medium onion
- 1 can tomato sauce or gluten free enchilada sauce
- salt and pepper, to taste
- 1 tsp cumin
- 1/2 tsp oregano
- 1 tsp chili powder
- 1/2 tsp garlic
- 1 can gluten free refried beans
- 3/4 cup aged cheddar cheese, grated
- 12 whole gluten free tortillas
- cilantro, chopped

optional fillings
mexican rice
plain kefir
guacamole
green chilies
pico de gallo

Brown ground beef with onion and season to taste. Add spices. Cook for 2 minutes. Pour in sauce and simmer over low heat. Add 1/4 cup water if mixture gets too dry.

Heat refried beans in a saucepan. Add cheese and stir in till melted. Keep warm.

Heat tortillas in microwave for one minute.

Spread a small amount of beans on each tortilla. Add meat. Fold over ends, then roll up. Place two burritos on a microwave-safe plate. Drizzle sauce over the top and sprinkle with more grated cheddar. Microwave for one minute or until cheese is melted and burritos are very hot. Serve immediately.

mexican rice

- 1 tbs olive oil
- 2 cloves garlic, minced
- 1 onion, diced
- 1 1/2 cups basmati rice
- 1 8 oz can tomato sauce
- 1 1/2 cups vegetable broth
- 1 cup corn kernels
- 1/2 cup diced carrots
- 1/2 cup frozen peas
- 1/4 tsp chili powder
- 1/4 tsp cumin
- Kosher salt and freshly ground black pepper, to taste
- 2 roma tomatoes, diced
- 2 tbs chopped fresh cilantro leaves

Heat olive oil in a large skillet over medium heat. Add garlic and onion, and cook, stirring frequently, until onions have become translucent, about 2-3 minutes. Stir in rice until toasted, about 2 minutes.

Stir in tomato sauce and vegetable broth, and bring to a simmer, about 2 minutes. Stir in corn, carrots, peas, chili powder and cumin; season with salt and pepper to taste. Bring to a boil; cover, reduce heat and simmer until rice is cooked through, about 13-16 minutes. Stir in tomatoes.

Serve immediately, garnished with cilantro, if desired.

chopsticks and rice

- 3 cups cooked jasmine rice
- 3 tbs sesame oil
- 1 cup frozen peas and carrots (thawed)
- 1 small onion, chopped
- 2 tsp minced garlic
- 2 eggs, slightly beaten
- 1/4 cup gluten free soy sauce

Optional - 2 cups cooked chicken bites

On medium high heat, the oil in a large skillet or wok. Add the peas/carrots, onion and garlic. Stir fry until tender. Lower the heat to medium low and push the mixture off to one side, then pour your eggs on the other side of skillet and stir fry until scrambled.

Add the rice and soy sauce and chicken(optional). Blend all together. Stir fry until thoroughly heated.

sloppy joes

- 2 tbs coconut oil
- 2 lbs ground beef
- 1/2 large onion, diced
- 1 green bell pepper, diced
- 5 cloves garlic, minced
- 1 1/2 cups ketchup
- 1 cup water
- 2 tbs brown sugar
- 2 tsp chili powder
- 1 tsp dry mustard
- 1/2 tsp red pepper flakes
- 1 tbs worcestershire sauce
- 1 tomato chopped
- 1 chipotle, seeded and diced
- 1 tsp tabasco sauce
- salt to taste
- freshly ground black pepper, to taste
- gluten free buns

Add coconut oil to a large skillet or dutch oven over medium high heat. Add ground beef and cook until brown. Drain most of the fat and discard.

Add onions, green pepper, and garlic. Cook for a few minutes, or until vegetables begin to soften.

Add ketchup, brown sugar, chili powder, red pepper flakes, dry mustard, and water. Stir to combine and simmer for 15 minutes, adding salt and pepper to taste. Also, add tomato, chipotle, Worcestershire, and Tabasco if desired. Taste and adjust seasonings as needed.

hot ham and cheese

- 2 tbs unsalted butter
- 3 tbs gluten free all purpose flour
- 2 cups hot almond milk
- 1 tsp kosher salt
- 1/2 tsp ground black pepper
- Pinch of nutmeg
- 12 ounces Gruyère cheese, grated (5 cups)
- 1/2 cup freshly grated parmesan cheese
- 16 slices gluten free white sandwich bread, crusts removed
- gluten free dijon mustard
- 8 ounces baked virginia ham, sliced

Preheat oven to 400 degrees.

Melt the butter over low heat in a small saucepan and add the flour all at once, stirring with a wooden spoon for 2 minutes. Slowly pour the hot milk into the butter–flour mixture and cook, whisking constantly until the sauce is thickened. Off the heat add the salt, pepper, nutmeg, ½ cup grated Gruyère, and the Parmesan and set aside.

To toast the bread, place the slices on two baking sheets and bake for 5 minutes. Turn each slice and bake for another 2 minutes, until toasted.

Lightly brush half the toasted breads with mustard, add a slice of ham to each, and sprinkle with half the remaining Gruyère. Top with another piece of toasted bread. Slather the tops with the cheese sauce, sprinkle with the remaining Gruyère, and bake the sandwiches for 5 minutes. Turn on the broiler and broil for 3 to 5 minutes, or until the topping is bubbly and lightly browned. Serve hot.

tomato
carrot soup

- 6 tomatoes
- 3 carrots
- salt and pepper to taste
- 1 tbs braggs amino acids
- 1 tsp dried parsley
- 1 tbs olive oil

Juice the tomatoes and carrots. Add salt, pepper, amino acids, parsley and olive oil. Simmer for 10-15 minutes in a pot over medium-low heat.

taco
bar ideas

- Ground organic turkey or chicken sauteed with taco seasoning
- Sauteed mushrooms, sweet potato, and/or eggplant (in sea salt and oil of choice)
- Spaghetti squash
- Sliced jicama
- Roasted cauliflower puree
- Refried beans – black or pinto
- Fresh corn mixed with diced summer squash, saute for sweeter flavor
- Fresh pico de gallo salsa
- Guacamole
- Dairy-free cheese

taco seasoning

- 1 tbs chili powder
- 1/4 tsp garlic powder
- 1/4 tsp onion powder
- 1/4 tsp red pepper flakes
- 1/4 tsp oregano
- 1/4 tsp paprika
- 1 1/2 tsp cumin
- 1 tsp salt
- 1 tsp black pepper

Mix all ingredients together and store in air tight container.

To use, mix 2 lbs of ground beef when browning meat in skillet on stove top.

sweet potato taters

- 2 lbs sweet potatoes
- 2 tbs olive oil
- 1/8 tsp salt
- 1/8 tsp pepper
- 1/8 tsp garlic powder
- 1/8 tsp paprika

Preheat oven to 450 degrees.
Line a baking sheet with parchment paper or silpat.

In a shallow dish, combine oil and spices.

If leaving the skin on, scrub your sweet potatoes really well. If not, peel your potatoes. Cut sweet potatoes into 1/4" fries.

Toss fries in olive oil to coat. Spread fries out on a prepared baking sheet.

Bake for 20 minutes, turning occasionally or until fries are browned.

fish
sticks

- 4 fish fillets, cut into strips
- 1/2 cup cornmeal
- 1/4 cup gluten free all purpose flour
- 1/2 cup grated parmigiano-reggiano cheese
- 1 tsp lemon zest
- 1 egg
- 2 tbs oil

Combine cornmeal, flour, cheese and lemon zest on a plate. Whisk egg in another dish. Dip fish strips in egg and dredge through breading to coat the fish evenly. Preheat skillet to medium-high, add oil. Add the fish to the skillet and cook until golden brown on both sides, about 4 minutes per side.

chicken bites

- 4 large boneless skinless chicken breasts
- 4 tbs gluten free soy sauce
- 3 tsp graded ginger
- 2 cups corn starch
- oil - eye ball for frying

Cut your chicken into bite size pieces.

Mix your soy sauce and grated ginger together.

Marinade your chicken in soy sauce for about 20 minutes.

Then coat your chicken thoroughly in corn starch. You can use a brown paper bag and shake it to cover, much like you would fried chicken. Place the corn starch and chicken inside then roll top closed and shake it.

Cook your coated chicken individually in your fry pan with oil at 400 degrees (high heat).

Cook each piece in the oil for a few minutes on both sides.

Take your cooked chicken out and let them drip over baking rack (over cookie sheet lined with paper towels).

After they have dripped for a minute or two, place in oven to keep warm. Serve with your favorite sauce.

sausage
mac n' broccoli

- 2 cups water
- 2 cups rice milk
- 1 box gluten free macaroni
- 2 cups gluten free, lactose free cheese, shredded
- 1 tbs dijon mustard
- 4 gluten free polish sausages
- 2 cups chopped broccoli

Bring water and milk to a boil in a 2 quart pan. Add macaroni cook for 8 minutes. Then stir in shredded cheese and dijon mustard until cheese is all melted.

While macaroni is cooking; saute sausage.

Steam the broccoli.

Once the sausage is cooked, slice and stir into macaroni and cheese, along with broccoli.

Allow to sit for 5 minutes before serving.

crispy baked chicken legs

- 3-4 lbs chicken drumsticks or wings
- 1 tbs marjoram
- 2 tbs oregano
- 1 1/4 tsp smoked salt
- 1 1/2 tbs garlic powder
- 1 tsp paprika
- 1 tsp white pepper
- 1/2 tsp chipotle
- 1 chicken bouillon cube, crushed
- 2 tbs oil

Preheat oven to 425 degrees.

Place chicken in a large bowl with all the spices and crushed bouillon cube, and then drizzle with 2 tablespoons oil. Cover chicken completely with paste.

Line a baking pan with foil; top with a wire rack. Arrange chicken legs out in a single layer. While the chicken legs are baking, oil will slowly drip to the bottom of the baking pan.

Bake chicken legs until cooked through and skin is crispy, about 45-50 minutes. If cooking wings rotate half way through-roughly after 20 minutes. Rotate chicken drumsticks and cook an additional 30 minutes.

Remove and serve with yogurt sauce or african pepper sauce.

meatballs
and mashies

- 1 lb ground beef
- 1 1/4 tsp salt
- 1/4 tsp ground black pepper
- 1/2 cup chopped onion
- 1/2 cup chopped bell pepper
- 1 egg, lightly beaten
- 8 oz canned diced tomatoes, without juice
- 1/2 cup gluten free oats

Topping
- 1/3 cup ketchup
- 2 tbs brown sugar
- 1 tbs mustard

mashies
- 2 lbs potatoes
- 1 tbs salt
- 1 cup almond milk
- 4 tbs butter or Earth Balnce
- 1/4 tsp black pepper
- 1/4 tsp nutmeg

Preheat oven to 375 degrees.

Mix all meatball ingredients well. Form into 2 inch balls and place in a baking dish.

Topping:
Mix ingredients for topping and spread on meatballs. Bake for 1 hour.

Chop potatoes into large chunks.

Boil potatoes in large pot covered in water, till soft when poked with a fork, about 30 minutes.

Drain potatoes. Place potatoes back in hot pan, add salt, milk, butter, pepper and nutmeg. Mash with potato masher or whip with electric mixer on low.

meatballs
and spaghetti

- 2 lbs ground pork
- 1/2 cup gluten free bread crumbs
- 1 tbs italian seaoning
- 2 eggs
- salt and pepper to taste
- 1 package gluten free spaghetti noodles
- 1 16oz jar gluten free marinara sauce

Mix ground pork, eggs, bread crumbs, italian seasoning, salt and pepper in medium bowl. Form into two inch meatballs. Fill the bottom of a large crockpot with water. Place meatballs in crockpot and cook on high for 4 hours or low for 8 hours.

Prepare spaghetti noodles as per package instructions. Heat sauce in small pan on stove top.

Serve spaghetti topped with meatballs and sauce.

lillie
lasagna

- 9 no-bake gluten free lasagna noodles
- 1/4 cup butter
- 1 tsp minced garlic
- 1/4 cup gluten free all purpose flour
- 1 tsp salt
- 1 tsp pepper
- 1 cup chicken broth
- 1 cup almond milk
- 2 cups mozzarella cheese, divided
- 1/2 cup fresh grated parmesan, divided
- 1 tbs Italian seasoning
- 1 cup ricotta
- 1 1/2 cups cooked shredded chicken
- 1 cup fresh baby spinach

Preheat oven to 350 degrees.

Lightly mist an 8"x8" dish with cooking spray. Set aside.

Pre-cook the lasagna noodles by boiling for 4 minutes.

Melt the butter in a medium saucepan. Add garlic. Cook until fragrant. Stir in the flour, salt, and pepper. Cook for 1 minute. Mix in the chicken broth and milk. Simmer until slightly thickened and remove from heat.

Stir in 1 cup mozzarella, ¼ cup of the parmesan and Italian seasoning.

Pour 1/3 of your sauce mixture into your prepared pan. Layer the noodles followed by the ricotta, chicken, and fresh spinach. Smother in 1/3 of the sauce and repeat the layers once more.

Top with the remaining noodles, sauce, and cheese.

Bake covered for 40 minutes or until hot and bubbly. Remove foil until cheese is brown.

mama mia lasagna

- 9 no-bake gluten free lasagna noodles
- 1/2 cup onion, chopped
- 2 cloves garlic, minced
- 1/2 cup celery, chopped
- 1/4 cup butter
- 1 tsp sea salt
- 1 lb ground pork
- 1 tbs Italian seasoning
- 1 jar 15oz marinara sauce
- 1 cup ricotta cheese
- 1/2 cup grated parmesan cheese
- 1/2 cup fresh spinach
- 3 cups mozzarella cheese

Preheat oven to 350 degrees.

Lightly mist an 8"x8" dish with cooking spray. Set aside.

Pre-cook the lasagna noodles by boiling for 4 minutes.

In a skillet over medium-high heat, melt butter and saute onions, celery, and garlic for 2 minutes. Stir in ground pork, Italian seasoning and cook until brown, stirring frequently. Add the marinara sauce and cook on low for 10 minutes, stirring occasionaly.

Lightly coat bottom of pan with marinara mixture. Layer lasagna strips over the sauce. Top with about a third of the cheeses and spinach. Once again layer with marinara mixture, a layer of lasagna strips, a third of the cheese. For the final layer, use the remaining lasagna strips. Top with rest of marinara and shredded cheese.

Cover with foil and bake for 40 minutes. Remove foil and bake for 10 minutes until cheese is golden. Let stand for 15 minutes before serving.

Mom Certified spice

- 2 1/2 tbs paprika
- 2 tbs sea salt
- 2 tbs garlic powder
- 1 tbs black pepper
- 1 tbs onion powder
- 1 tbs cayenne pepper
- 1 tbs dried oregano
- 1 tbs dried thyme

Combine all ingredients thoroughly. Store in air tight container.

You're allowed
to scream,
You're allowed
to cry,
but do not give up.

chipotle mayo

- 1 1/2 tsp chipotles
- 3/4 cup mayo

Slice chipotles in half and scrape out seeds. Discard seeds and dice chipotles.

Mix diced chipotles with mayo. Store in airtight container in refrigerator.

sweet onion dip

- 1 tbs butter
- 1 medium sweet onion, peeled and sliced
- 2 tbs cider vinegar
- 2 tbs honey
- 1 tbs mustard
- 1 cup mayonnaise
- salt and pepper to taste

Melt butter in a medium frying pan over moderate heat and add the sliced onions. Cook, stirring occasionally, until the onions soften, then caramelize. This should take between 10 to 15 minutes. The lower the heat, the longer it takes, but the less likely you are to burn the onions.

Once the onions are a medium brown, remove from heat and add the vinegar.

Place the onions and vinegar into a small food processor. Add the honey and mustard, and process or blend until smooth.

Add the mayonnaise and salt and pepper to taste, stirring to combine. Refrigerate covered, until ready to serve.

ginger honey

- 1/2 cup honey
- 2 tbs gluten free soy sauce
- 1 tbs minced onion
- 2 tbsp ketchup
- 1 tbs oil
- 1/2 tsp garlic powder

Add all ingredients to a small sauce pan.

Mix your honey sauce and simmer over medium heat for ten minutes, until it starts to bubble and/or becomes thick.

honey mustard

- 3 tbs dijon mustard
- 1 1/2 tbs honey

Mix the two ingredients together. Store in an air tight container up to one week in the refrigerator.

boys will be boys

garlic aioli

- 1/2 cup mayo
- 3 cloves garlic, pressed
- 1 tbs lemon juice
- 1 tsp dijon mustard
- 1/2 tsp tarragon

Combine all ingredients and refrigerate for at least 1 hour before serving. Store covered in refrigerator for up to 3 days.

8 Benefits of Baking with Kids

1. Builds Math Skills

2. Enriches Oral Vocabulary

3. Teaches Scientific Concepts

4. Boosts Reading Skills

5. Introduces Life Skills

6. Develops Fine Motor Skills

7. Promotes Social Skills

8. Provides Fun "Connect" Time!

the most memorable days usually end with the dirtiest clothes.

GF Mom
flour blend

- 1/3 cup white rice flour
- 3 tbs cornstarch
- 3 tbs brown rice flour
- 3 tbs tapioca starch
- 2 tbs + 2 tsp gluten free dry milk powder
- 1 tsp potato starch
- 1 1/2 tsp xanthum gum

Sift ingredients together and store in an air tight container.

Package up a few cups and give as a gift to fellow gluten free bakers.

Food Feeds Fertility

Infertility is an issue that plagues many women every year. But, did you know that this is a condition that can also be misdiagnosed where the very foods that you eat are the root of the problem? It makes me wonder how many families spend an astounding amount of money on unnecessary medical bills only to be left with their questions unanswered. Can it be as simple as food?

I would like to introduce all of you to a woman who is living proof that, indeed, the foods that you eat can cause infertility. I found her story so inspiring that I want to share it with all of you. Please welcome my guest Tiffany Hinton.

Tiffany helps people every day. Her website GF Mom Certified is chock full of information, reading materials, recipes and her own personal story of how she and her husband overcame many years of an infertility diagnosis.

Why did you begin doing this? I started GF Mom Certified for my girls. As a mom with two little girls with severe food allergies and being gluten and dairy free myself, I know the fear and anxiety a mom faces when trying to feed her children. Food is so ingrained in our culture for rewards, celebrations and more, that the idea of not being able to share with others broke my heart. I wanted my girls to grow up eating the same things I did. I love our old family favorites like my grandmother's chocolate pie or Grandma Pecola's sweet potato pie.

How long did it take you to receive a correct diagnosis? I am still struggling today with being fully diagnosed by my medical team of doctors. After almost fourteen years of believing I had ulcerative colitis, IBS, asthma and several other issues including unexplained infertility, my reproductive endocrinologists found that I was positive for the celiac antibodies. Going gluten free has restored my good health. My most recent endoscopy and colonoscopy show blunted villi and damage, although I am not positive for the DQ-2 or DQ-8 (the most common genes associated with celiac). My gastro intestinal doctor will not diagnose me. My gluten free lifestyle has given me my three girls, and a healthy and vibrant life. I have been off all of my prescribed medications for six years. I believe you have to fight for a solution and find the source of the ailment, not mask the symptoms with medicine. So, if you are still struggling as you read this, know there is hope.

What would you tell others that have similar symptoms? If you suffer from celiac symptoms, you need to be tested before going gluten free. Ask for a blood panel and biopsy. I encourage you to find a doctor who listens to you and is willing to investigate the cause. The best advice I received from my OB/GYN several years ago was that they could not help and to find a specialist that I liked. He told me to interview them like I would as if I was hiring them for a job. Take a list of questions to ask.

How long have you been GF Mom Certified? I launched GF Mom Certified in 2012 after my first daughter was diagnosed with galactosemia* at three days old and we needed to feed her to keep her alive. I had to learn to prepare food she would eat without dairy and after her gluten reaction at eighteen months old while traveling. I converted my blog and launched our website to provide gluten and dairy free kitchen solutions to others that are "Mom Certified" and "Kid Approved". Our first cookbook was published in April 2012.

Where do you get your inspiration for your recipes? Most of my inspiration comes from old family recipes. I love food. I love how food can bring a family together, how food can break down barriers and I love how food can fill a room with joy and laughter.

Where do you typically eat out? We live in the Chicagoland area which is a blessing when it comes to choices. Personally, I love PF Changs. We also eat out at a few chains like Noodles & Company, Go Roma, Five Guys, Jason's Deli and a local Mexican dive.**

What types of people come to you for help and advice? We attract what we are is so true. I talk to moms and people struggling with infertility the most. I am open and love to share. At a recent book signing, there was a mom of two autistic children in tears because she did not know that you could still have some of your comfort food that are gluten and dairy free. Our cookbooks bring normalcy back after years of struggling to figure out what to feed our children.

Do you attend many events or speaking engagements? I love to attend and speak at events. You can find us all over the nation from California to North Carolina and most definitely in the Chicago area. We keep a list of upcoming events on our website at **gfmomcertified.com**. I love to answer questions, so if you find us at an event ask away. If we don't know the answer, I will help you find someone who does. The gluten free community sticks together and helps each other.

Where do you hope this will lead? I want to be able to do what I love full time. What is that you ask? I want to be able to cook and dream in my kitchen designing recipes day in and day out. I would love to have a New York Times best-selling cookbook but more importantly, it is about helping moms by taking away the fear.

Where can we find all of your information and products? GF Mom Certified products and information can be found online at our website http://gfmomcertified.com on Twitter at @gfmomcertified and Facebook. Our cookbooks can be found online at Amazon, BarnesandNoble.com and our website. You can find our cookbooks in several grocery stores in the Chicago area and Northwest Indiana including Strack & Van Til, Ultra Foods, Fresh Thyme and a few Hy-Vee stores.

Thank you Tiffany for sharing your story with us! I appreciate your willingness to help others from your own experiences. I have to add that it was a pleasure meeting you and your husband and discussing what brought you both to what you are doing now. Your passion is evident and I know you will continue to grow that passion into even bigger ventures in the future.

As for Tiffany's thoughts on how food brings us together, I completely agree. Because most of the time we are all trying to deny that food should be in every part of our lives and I don't believe this to be true, healthy or realistic. I have said it before and I will say it again -

*Galactosemia is a disorder that effects how the body processes galactose, a simple sugar.
** These restaurants may not be safe for your family's allergies needs. As always, please check their menu options and ingredients to be safe.

- Written by Tracy Bush, Nutrimom - Food Allergy Liason
(336) 486-1905
www.AllergyPhoods.com

BEHIND EVERY YOUNG
CHILD WHO BELIEVES
IN HIMSELF IS A
PARENT WHO
BELIEVED FIRST

Grocery Shopping Ideas

Veggies

Asparagus
Baby spinach
Basil
Beets
Bell peppers
Broccoli
Carrots
Cauliflower
Celery
Cucumber
Dill
Garlic
Kale
Onions
Potatoes
Romaine lettuce
Rosemary
Sage
Snap peas
Spring mix
Squash
Sweet Potatoes
Tomatoes

Meats

Bison
Chicken breast
Ground pork
Ground turkey
Lamb
Tuna
Wild caught fish

Fruits

Apples
Avocados
Bananas
Blueberries
Grapes
Lemons
Limes
Pears
Pineapples
Strawberries

Non-dairy

Almond milk
Canned coconut milk
Coconut ice cream
Coconut yogurt

Baking

Baking powder
Baking soda
Corn starch
Egg replacer
Non-dairy powdered milk
Potato starch
Rice flour
Steel cut oats
Tapioca flour
Xantham gum

Snacks

Carrot sticks
Pineapples
Popsicles
Tortilla chips

Condiments/Oils

100% maple syrup
Apple cider vinegar
Balsamic vinegar
Coconut oil
Dijon mustard
Ghee
Grapeseed oil
Olive oil
Red wine vinegar
Rice vinegar

Spices

Bay leaf
Black pepper
Chili powder
Cumin
Curry powder
Garlic powder
Ginger
Nutmeg
Onion powder
Oregano
Rosemary
Sea salt
Tumeric
Vanilla extract

Nuts/Seeds

Almonds
Almond butter
Chia seeds
Ground flax
Pecans
Pumpkin seeds
Sun butter
Sunflower seeds
Tahini
Walnuts

Canned Goods

Black beans
Chick peas
Coconut milk
Diced tomatoes
Organic broths
Unsweetened applesauce

Miscellaneous

Apple butter
Cocoa powder
Honey
Jam
Pumpkin puree
Tea

Meal planning has saved our family money and helped to create an easy plan to follow with our busy schedule. I take about 30 minutes every two weeks to plan the meals for the next two weeks, then make a corresponding grocery list. Personally, I shop at 2 grocery stores, one European market for produce and meat; and one whole and fresh market store for gluten free and organic pantry items. I have a base shopping list we use, then I add additional items based on the meals planned. In our house the planned meal is either made for lunch, then re-served at supper time; or vice versa the planned meal is served at supper time and the leftovers are used for lunch the following day. If you find an item on the menu and the recipe is not contained in Kid Approved it will be found in Mom Certified Celebrated Heritage or on our website. *Our goal is to make cooking for your kids simple and easy, allowing you to bring fun back to your kitchen and smiles to your table with every meal.*

weekly
menu option 1

apples	Fri - pizza
bananas	Sat - chicken legs and fries
strawberries	Sun - liver burgers and cabbage with
Pineapples	fries
avocados	Mon - whole chicken and veggies
limes	Tues - spaghetti and meatballs
oranges	Wed - bison burgers
peaches	Thurs - potato soup and sandwiches
pears	Fri - pizza
romaine lettuce	Sat - chicken bites and rice
tomatoes	Sun - breakfast for lunch
green peppers	Mon - hotdogs and fries
onions	Tues - cowboy chili mix
bag of potatoes	Wed - lasagna with fresh mozzarella
sweet potatoes	and spinach
frozen veggies (peas/	Thurs - leftovers
carrots)	
butter (2)	
eggs (2)	
16 chicken legs	
24 hotdogs	
1 lb pepperoni	
1 lb canadian bacon	
1 lb gypsy bacon	
mozzarella sliced	
2 hunks of mozzarella	
fresh mozzarella	
(5 balls)	

weekly menu option 2

apples
bananas
strawberries
Pineapple (2)
avocados
limes
pears
romaine lettuce
tomatoes
green peppers
onions
bag of potatoes
sweet potatoes
frozen veggies (peas/carrots)
butter (2)
eggs (1)
ground pork (2)
ground chicken (2)
grass fed burgers
mahi mahi 3
swordfish 3
12 hotdogs
2 lb krakus ham
1 lb pepperoni
1 lb canadian bacon
2 lb gypsy bacon
mozzarella sliced
2 hunks of mozzarella
fresh mozzarella (5 balls)
gf spaghetti (2)
gf flour
sweet potato flour

Fri - pizza
Sat - sandwiches and soup
Sun - tacos
Mon - whole chicken, mashies & veggies
Tues - sandwiches/chips lunch - chicken bites/sweet potato fries
Wed - spaghetti
Thurs - hamburgers and mashies, veggies
Fri - banana muffins & pizza
Sat - spaghetti and meatballs
Sun - pancakes, parfaits, chicken legs & fries
Mon - sausage mac 'n' cheese
Tues - sandwiches/chips/fruit - sloppy joes
Wed - chicken and rice, chili cheese dogs
Thurs - fish, rice and curry
Fri - pizza, pretzel dogs

weekly
menu option 3

apples
bananas
strawberries
Pineapple
avocados
limes
romaine lettuce
tomatoes
onions
bag of potatoes
sweet potatoes
frozen veggies(peas/
carrots)
butter (2)
eggs (2)
whole chicken
2 lb ground chicken (2)
16 chicken legs
1 lb canadian bacon
1 lb gypsy bacon
mozzarella sliced
2 hunks of mozzarella
fresh mozzarella
(5 balls)
canned coconut milk (6)
hot dogs
kobe dogs
bacon
hamburgers
hot dog buns
pepperoni
gf spaghetti
gf pizza crust
taco shells
refried beans
cereal
white rice flour
brown rice flour
zanthum gum

Fri - pizza
Sat - chili cheese dogs, hot dogs,
fries
Sun - breakfast for lunch
(pancakes, apples, eggs, fruit,
bacon)
Mon - whole chicken and mashies,
veggies
Tues - sandwiches and fruit
Wed - hotdogs and fries, veggies
Thurs - chicken legs and fries
Fri - pizza
Sat - chicken legs
Sun - chicken tacos
Mon - spaghetti and meatballs
Tues - sandwiches, fruit, chips
Wed - pizza lunch
Thurs -hamburgers, fries
Fri - pizza

Breakfast options - pancakes,
cereal, oatmeal, eggs, bacon, fruit,
muffins,

AKA I'm Gluten

GLUTENS

Barley
Beers
Bulgur
Cereal Filler
Couscous
Dextrins
Durum Flour
Farina
Graham Flour
Kamut
Lagers
Natural Flavors
Malt Flavoring
Maltodextrins
Modified Food Starch
Modified Starch
Monosodium Glutamate
Rusk
Rye
Semolina
Soy Sauce
Spelt
Thickening Bran
Triticale
Wheat
Wheat Flour
Wheat Germ
Wheat Germ Oil

SUGARS

Corn Syrup
Dextrose
Fructose
Fruit Sugar
Glucose
Glucose Syrup
Golden Syrup
Honey
Invert Sugar
Malt Syrup
Maple Syrup
Molasses
Sucrose
Sugar
Treacle

DAIRY

Casein
Caseinates
Ghee
Hydrolized Casein
Lactose
Milk Solids
Non-Milk Fat Solids
Skimmed Milk Powder
Whey
Whey Powder
Whey Proteins & Sugars
Yogurt

gluten free
travel tips

Do you ever worry about traveling? Do you fret about what you are going to eat? or where? If you travel like I do, traveling gluten free is just a part of life.

Here are my top 5 tips for traveling gluten free

1. Research
- Look up where you are going including the hotel and local restaurants. I love using yelp to read the reviews. For example type in "yelp: gluten free pizza LA Downtown". This will bring what offers a gluten free pizza crust and also vegan cheese. I quickly scan through the reviews to see if any one has gotten sick from the food. If the restaurant has great reviews from other gluten free people, then it's a go!

2. Favorites
- If you travel frequently make a list of favorites in the cities you go to most often. This makes the trip fun and relaxing. For instance when we travel to Charlotte we always eat at Kings Kitchen that has an amazing gluten free southern food menu. You can also rely on the large chain restaurants in the bigger cities like PF Changs or Flemings. For more restaurant ideas visit GF Mom Certified's Eating Out page.

3. Snacks
- Pack your snacks for the flight or drive. I suggest protein bars and fruit. One of my favorites are Kind bars. You can also find these at Starbucks when you are out. Apples and cuties make great fruit to travel with because it is hard to bruise and packs well. You could also throw some peanuts or dried fruit in your purse.

4. Speak Up and Ask
- When you are visiting a new restaurant or hotel, ask if they have a gluten free menu or suggestions. Once the staff knows you are gluten free or have an allergy I find most are extremely helpful with making suggestions or offering substitutes. Many hotels will even change up your welcome gift to a gluten free option.

5. Relax
- Once you have an idea of where you are eating and all the options in the area relax and enjoy your trip. Remember you can always use Bing on your phone for a quick solution.

About the Author

According to my daughter's view of what I do, "You help daddy use paper, color, and make supper for work and [you] work in the downstairs office with the computer."

Through the eyes of a child what I do seems simplistic and fun. In reality, it is also work but super fun. I am Tiffany Hinton, a gluten free lifestyle expert and super mom to 3 magical little girls. I love to spend hours in my kitchen dreaming of food and flavors. The challenge which presented itself several years ago was creating great tasting food that was also safe for our family. As a mom with gluten intolerance and with children who react to gluten, can't breakdown dairy and have a peanut allergy, I really understand the importance of having safe food options that are easy and convenient for the busy parent.

I grew up in my grandmother's kitchen and used my 30 plus years of cooking and baking experience in the creation of GF Mom Certified. In our most recent cookbook, "Mom Certified Celebrates Heritage", we spent over 2 years recreating the recipes that my husband and I grew up eating. My husband's family is originally from the south and I grew up in the rural midwest. Just think of it as "gluten free meets country/ soul food". The cookbook includes over 100 recipes that are not only gluten and dairy free, but also most are soy and peanut free. Recipes include sweet potato pie, fried chicken, collard greens, goulash and many more family historical favorites interwoven with family snapshots and stories.

GF Mom Certified allows me to turn my passion for cooking into gluten free kitchen solutions for others including our cookbooks, free weekly recipes, recipe conversions (by special request), blogs, and educational classes. My typical day includes time spent with my girls allowing our creativity to flow as we enjoy art, time outdoors along with fun kitchen projects. Some of our most fun moments have been caught on video for our GF Mom youtube channel. I have heard many say they watch

SHE'S PRECIOUS

to the King of Kings, so don't you
dare underestimate the plans that He
has for her, because they are great.

our kitchen videos just to see what Franki is going to do next, like the time she licked the sprinkles off the cookies we were decorating or introduced the world to 'monkey' her little buddy.

I love working with fellow moms and showing them that life with food allergies doesn't have to be scary or filled with anxiety. Some of the simplest tricks can bring normalcy back to a family, such as gf stickers in the kitchen and just knowing what to eat instead of focusing on what you cannot eat. Food brings emotion and memories from those special times in life. For me, I will always remember my Grandma's chocolate pie. I may not be able to eat it the way grandma made it but that does not mean I can never eat it again or that it won't taste fabulous. "It's magnificent", according to my husband. With a few simple substitutes it still has the same flavor and I can enjoy the moments I remember at my grandma's kitchen table with cold chocolate pie and can tell my girls how grandma used to cut me a slice of pie after school. I would walk to her house and she would serve it up with a big scoop of cool whip or melted toasted meringue. I encourage you to find us online and bring fun back into your kitchen! G-free style of course.

Tiffany Hinton is an Author, Blogger, Public Speaker, Cook and Advocate for the Gluten-Free community. She has written 7 cookbooks.

She has spoken at several Gluten & Allergen Free Expos. And, Tiffany has participated in gluten free events at grocery stores in the Midwest where she has cooked and handed out gluten free samples in their Organic Produce Departments.

Tiffany has a compelling story that led to her gluten free lifestyle. She is not your average author and is a Person You Should Know. Tiffany is available for speaking engagements, book readings/signings, cooking demonstrations, as well as gluten and allergy free promotional events. She would be thrilled to work with any company that instills the same healthy lifestyle that she, the Gluten-Free Mom, promotes.

Gluten Free Resources

EnerG
5960 1st Ave. South
Seattle, WA 98108
www.ener-g.com

Freedom Foods
855.909.1717
www.freedomfoodsus.com

GF Harvest
578 Lane 9
Powell, WY 82435
www.gfharvest.com

Namaste Food, LLC
PO Box 3133
Coeur d'Alene, ID 83816
www.namstefoods.com

Now Real Food
Bloomingdale, IL 60108
www.nowrealfood.com

SunButter LLC
PO Box 3022
Fargo, ND 58108
www.sunbutter.com

Virtuous Living
PO Box 6538
Upper Marlboro, MD 20792
www.virtuousliving.com

Wildree
555 Jefferson Blvd
Warwick, RI 02886
www.wildtree.com

Zocalo
Lynnwood, WA 98087
www.culinarycollective.com

Index

Reviews

You are my inspiration. I am back in the kitchen today....we are blessed with many leftovers.
- Elizabeth Gronert

I'm so excited! I am still learning how to bake gluten-free for myself and my family. This will help so much.
- Robin Lehman

This is the book I gave my kids. Her directions are easy enough for any 4th grader to follow andmake. My kids made her meringues with only limited help after getting meringue all over the bottom of my oven. (Don't ask!)
- fearlessdining.com

I figured if it was half as good as her first cookbook then I'd love it. Well, I'm excited to say that, in my opinion, it's even better!....
- Lauren Kossack

If you or someone you know is allergic to Gluten this book is a must have item in your kitchen. I am not a chef by any means but this book has the easiest recipes.
- Stephanie Person

As a
Thank You

CLAIM YOUR FREE
60
Pages of Recipes

http://thanks.gfmomcertified.com

CPSIA information can be obtained at www.ICGtesting.com
Printed in the USA
BVIW12n0854030517
482974BV00010B/107